APPLIED PSYCHOLOGY:

PRACTICAL GUIDE TO THE HUMAN MIND | STEP-BY-STEP ADVICE TO THE UNDERSTANDINGS OF PSYCHOLOGY

I0420710

JONNY BELL

Copyright © 2013 by Jonny Bell

WHY I WROTE THIS BOOK

Various psychology books are in the market. However, most of these books discuss theories and concepts in a complicated manner, which makes it difficult for people to understand. Now, people think that Psychology is only for a few but this broad field is so simple that it doesn't take a degree or a Ph. D. to understand.

I made this book to help you see the many applications of this field. From how you eat, think and act, elements of Psychology are there. It is an invisible factor in everything that we do. This eBook is easy to read and comprehend. I did my best to minimize any jargon that confuse, and replaced them with brief explanation that even a layman can understand.

Enjoy!

WHY YOU SHOULD READ THIS BOOK

Psychology is a broad field that deals with behavior and the faculty of thought. People complain about stress, problems and illnesses. Although medicine has greatly helped our woes, the way we act and think could help as well.

A deeper understanding of how we think and act will help you. After reading this eBook you will think twice about every action you do.

When you go to the doctor the cause of sickness is often physical, yet Psychology explains that there are invisible factors that are as much as important as tangible ones.

A refined version of the abstract studies of Psychology can help us have a better idea of how our mind functions.

TABLE OF CONTENTS

However vague the definition of morality, it is evidently the very source of the energy of our superego. The effects of these sets of rules are so great that an individual who thinks that he violated them would inflict self-punishment, event to the point of suicide, because of a feeling of guilt imposed by super ego.

Another aspect of genetics, a separate and equally different discipline, the epigenetics, is gaining popularity among experts. Epigenetics is a discipline that deals with the inheritable changes that happen in gene activity which are not caused by a change in DNA sequence. Changes in gene expression, or changes that allow a part of the gene to be suppressed or expressed, determine the

Applied Psychology

CHAPTER 1.

YOU ARE WHAT YOU THINK

Depression, anxiety and phobias are common psychological illnesses that people have. The common remedy for these are conventional drugs that alter our thought process. However, a more effective way to cure these is just by thinking the right thoughts.

Too much emphasis is given to physical cures that we forget that behavioral disorders are manifestations of something wrong in our psyche. Drugs are a problem-solution mismatch; changing how we think is the right cure.

In the mid-1900s Albert Ellis and Aaron Beck pioneered the **Cognitive Behavior Therapy (CBT)** as a method in treating psychological disorders.

UNDERSTANDING CBT

CBT runs under the premise that our thoughts play a vital part in the behavior that we express. Negative ideas about yourself can contribute to low self-esteem and self-pity. Our irrational behaviors on fears are made possible by how we think. CBT cures by changing our perception about these things. The therapy is goal oriented for it only focuses on one specific objective that can vary from person to person.

Albert Ellis argues that people do not fear objects, events or ideas but their perception about those. He emphasized that **irrational thinking** is the cause of phobias. Ellis cures by disputing these irrational thoughts and later making the patient realize the fault in reasoning.

Aaron Beck, on the other hand, focuses on **hasty generalizations** that cause people to lose value in themselves. Cutting down the fallacious generalizations can make the person realize that the generalization is actually just a single occurrence.

An example of how CBT works is how it treats people with Hydrophobia (fear of water). People thinking too much about water associate it with drowning thus making them anxious over the sight of water. CBT eliminates this fear by removing the root idea that water always kills.

Another, is how a teen girl generalizes that all of her classmates are prettier than her. The therapist questions this generalization until the patient realizes that not everyone is prettier.

DEALING WITH DEPRESSION, ANXIETY AND PHOBIAS

Depression anxiety and phobias all root from certain perceptions and expectations. Absolute statements like "I need to get perfect on this test," or "I should weigh less than 60 kilos," are thoughts that affect us. Not meeting these expectations causes depression and anxiety. Repeatedly getting hurt by these events escalates into a pure phobia.

The key to overcoming phobias is by disputing the absolute statements behind them and proving them false.

Albert Ellis explains how this happens by using the ABC model:

Activating event – this is a significant event that happens to the patient

Beliefs – the patient creates an association or a meaning from the event

Consequence- this the reaction to the belief that can be through phobias or anxiety attacks.

Ellis then creates a set of steps to combat these consequences.

1. **Know the cause**
   Find the reason why you get anxious or fearful. Irrational ideas are common hindrances for us to attain happiness. The following are common examples:

   > *I need to be an honors student to make my parents proud because if I'm not my parents will be ashamed.*

   > *In order to be called beautiful I have to be thin, because if I'm not then I'll be ugly.*

   > *I should be rich by 25 because it would be too late after that.*

   According to Ellis events aren't the cause of phobias but the backlashes behind them. To track down these causes you should put every thought on a diary. Whether or not the thought is positive or negative, a diary can help you log and keep track of your anxieties. For phobias, write the things that make you uncomfortable.

If you find it difficult to write all the time you can record yourself in an audio diary. You must exert effort in identifying every single cause. Anxieties often happen because of one thing. It is common that out of the many entries you write only one might be the main reason.

2. **Question the validity of the causes**

The next step is asking yourself if the causes have any relation to your life. Ask yourself if it is a big deal. Contradict the absolute statement by reversing it. If you believe that you have to be an honor student or have a high paying job to make your parents proud, ask the critical question of "does it even matter if I'm not?" Even if you aren't an honor student yet still you manage to graduate, would your parents still be proud? If you aren't a CEO but you work hard, would that cause your parents to disown you? Realizing that not having any of those things will make you less of a person is a step closer to freeing yourself.

This is very challenging but not impossible. Illogical reasoning is just caused by habit. Ask a friend to become your therapist to help you.

You can handover your diary or recordings to your friend and have your beliefs questioned. Your friend must be honest to help you. Bluntly telling you that your reasoning is fallacious will let you realize the errors.

It will be hard at first, but eventually after repeatedly telling yourself of the invalidity of your ideas you will change your views.

3. **Learn and apply**

    After changing your perception it's now time to confront your fears. When you encounter ideas that trigger you anxiety, think about all the things you learned in the treatment. If you are successful then you have just removed your anxiety or phobia. If not, you should try the therapy again from the start.

PRACTICAL APPROACH

Your fulfillment in life greatly depends on your level of empowerment. It depends on your knowledge of how much of your life you can control; how much of it you believe you can take charge of.

It is helplessness that brings about the greatest frustration in a person's life. It is what breaks the human spirit. It is what causes depression.

When a person starts thinking that there is nothing he can do to change his circumstance, he becomes a victim. Sad and powerless, he becomes stuck in a downward abyss, unable to seek help; unable to move forward.

No matter what the circumstance, you must learn to develop a sense of control.

Remember that there are two types of environments – the outside environment, and the inside environment.

The outside environment is difficult to control as there are many factors that affect it. You cannot control the weather. You cannot control time. You cannot control other people. The outside environment is something, which you need to learn to accept, something which you need to learn to predict. The outside environment is sometimes beautiful, but sometimes, it can also be unkind. Whatever it brings you, remember: you need to develop a sense of control.

You develop this sense of control by understanding the strength and impact of your inside environment. Your inside environment is something you can completely take charge of. Composed of your attitudes and behaviors, your inside environment is where you make your decisions and build your personality. It determines who you are, and what you decide to do.

The idea of taking charge is truly very simple, but it takes emotional maturity and effort. Making good decisions requires wisdom, and being in control requires composure, patience, optimism, confidence and self-belief.

CHAPTER 2.

IT'S ALL IN THE MIND

CBT only solves problems that are raised by habit. However, there are things you just can't avoid happening. Anxiety when speaking in public or taking an exam is an experience we all have gone through. You don't notice any factors or causes. It just simply happens.

For these problems that simply spring up, the solution lies in training our brains to recognize uncomfortable feelings and ignoring them. **Neuro-linguistic programming (NLP)** taps how our mind functions by reception, recognition and reaction.

Everything we do whether good or bad has a corresponding mental picture. Humans receive this mental picture by our five senses. This is the **neurological component.**

After receiving the stimulus, our mind then gives a name to the feeling. **Linguistic** stands for the language that we associate for the stimulus. It's not limited to words like happy, sad or anxious. Linguistics can also be non-verbal.

Our reaction to that feeling is our **programming.** We might become anxious, elated or ecstatic.

NLP uses these concepts to change our behavior to become productive. By using NLP, you can block out any negative thoughts and replace it with a new positive one.

SWISH METHOD

The **Swish method** uses mind pictures to replace a negative memory with a positive one. This method is popularly known by the **swish** sounds that accompanies the switch.

1. **Identify the problem**

   Remember a stressful experience in your life. Think about why you have this feeling in the first place. Be specific of where and what are the factors that come into play. Write it down to make it easier.

2. **Draw a mental picture**

   Ponder on your feeling, make sure to receive all five senses associated with it. Make a representation in your brain. This is your **neurological component** working.

   An example is when you feel intimidated talking to your boss. You may see your employer's piercing eyes. You may feel beads of sweat on your eyebrows. The smell of his perfume is overwhelming. The voice is deep and commanding. The humid air is making your taste buds dry.

   Capture that exact moment and make sure to remember it.

3. **Give it a name**

   Once you have a mental picture, label it. Through **linguistics,** we can easily associate that mental picture. If we recall the name, the thought or mental pictures quickly pops into our head.

4. **Flash the picture repeatedly**
Let the feeling take over. Be it anxiety or fear, just let it flow. Do this repeatedly until you know for sure the sensation that comes with that thought.

5. **Remember happy times**
Do the same thing, but this time with a happy memory that made you smile. Give a mind picture, freeze it and label it.

6. **Recall the memories**
Imagine the two memories as picture frames. Remember the two memories. Close your eyes and imagine that the bad picture is in front of you while the good one at the bottom part.

7. **Swish them**
Count to three and then quickly switch the two pictures which will cause the positive picture to become bigger. As you switch make a **swish** sound. The sound serves as an association with the switch.

8. **Repeat**
Do this over and over again. Breathe deep whenever you perform every switch. Relax your brain so that the technique replaces the feeling associated with the bad memory.

The next time you encounter your boss, just breathe in and switch the feeling of anxiety with a picture of confidence. All it takes is to say the word **'swish.'**

HOW TO MAKE PEOPLE DO WHAT YOU WANT

Another application of NLP is by sending **imbedded suggestions.** By using various stimuli that are associated with positive feelings and thoughts, you can manipulate a person's reaction.

It might be hypnotism, but persuading people to do what you want is helpful in business especially in marketing and team management.

1. **Plan what you want to say**
   Think about the real message you want the person to receive. Make sure the message is phrased positively. Whether you want the person to buy a product or do business with you, make the suggestion clear so that the message won't be confusing.

2. **Think of an incentive**
   People will do something if there is a guarantee that they won't lose anything. Entice them by using words like "relax," "this is going to be fun," or "you are going to learn a lot here."

3. **Emphasize the message**
   While talking, emphasize the point you want to get across subtly. People don't notice, but our

minds place great importance on how a speech is delivered. We are most likely to remember parts of a conversation that involve changing of tones and gestures. You can also replace words that sound like the message to subliminally suggest an idea.

The following sentences are how to persuade people to buy plane tickets for a vacation:

"Hey, do you feel **stressed** and **frustrated?** That the pressure is just piling too much that you simply want to **leave** everything and get away? Why not **pack your bags** now and **leave** everything behind. Fly away. Have an adventure. Chase happiness. "

Notice that the emphasized words suggest taking a plane for a vacation. To highlight the message even more, you can include simple and subtle gestures like a flick of the fingers or a raised eyebrow. Your voice modulation can make the person more receptive to the message. Be wary of overdoing it, because people might notice.

Do this repeatedly. Make frequent eye contact with the subject until you notice a change in body movement. If his body language makes a positive reaction to your embedded suggestion, this means that the subject has accepted the suggestion already.

These are only a few of the many methods utilizing the NLP approach. NLP can change a behavior of a person simply by inserting an association to a positive concept.

22

The techniques are usually used in business and human resources, but can also be applied to improve work habits. The two techniques are the most important since it deals about productivity and interactivity with people. They are also easy to learn but require lots of practice.

You can even create your own technique by applying the neurological, linguistic and programming concepts. NLP proves that problems and social interaction are all in the mind. Overcoming these obstacles just takes a change of perspective.

CHAPTER 3.

MIND AND BODY

So far we've discussed how the mind can influence our behavior. Physical factors also play a part in a healthy mind. After all, the mind can't function if the organs aren't doing their jobs.

Biopsychology is branch of psychology that deals with how the body contributes to the thought process and how it manifests through behavior.

Rene Descartes, a 17th century philosopher, argued that our human existence is based on the concept of **dualism.** Our minds and body are two separate entities that are interdependent of each other. Thus, one change in one component can also create changes in the other.

Only when it was in the 1949 did Biopsychology became a recognized field, when *The Organization of Behavior* was published in 1949 by Canadian psychologist Donald O. Hebb. His book theorized that brain activity affects our behavior. During his time it was believed that Psychology was so complicated that it would be impossible for any chemicals or biological concepts to play a part in the field.

FOOD FOR THOUGHTS

Whenever we eat, the components of our food are broken down and released. The chemicals are then injected into our bloodstream and eventually finds its way into the brain. What we eat definitely holds significance to our productivity and behavior. Here are a few tips whenever you think about eating:

1. **Cut the caffeine**

   A cup of Joe has been keeping the world awake for decades. But we've been taking too much caffeine.

   When the body works the brain neurons release a compound called **adenosine.** Once our body reaches an adenosine saturation point, we feel sleepy. Caffeine has compositions similar to adenosine. Instead of bonding with adenosine, caffeine clogs the receptors, making us unable to fall asleep.

   The bad thing about caffeine is that it creates **tolerance** within the brain. Soon, our brain will be searching for caffeine and might lead to caffeine addiction.

   Although Caffeine has been proven to help us be productive, creativity is sacrificed. Our output might increase but **increase** in **quality** hasn't been proven yet. **Balance** your caffeine intake to give you a boost. But make sure not to become dependent on it.

2. **Beer is good**

   Surprisingly, beer that has been notoriously known to cause traffic accidents, actually helps in becoming more creative. A reasonable amount jumpstarts our brain to its optimum capacity.

   The Cerebral cortex in our brain is in charge of

our thinking processes and consciousness. Once the beer kicks in, it loosens up the Cerebral cortex and removes all distractions. This frees up your mind and you begin thinking big ideas. Beer relaxes your brain to create space for creative thinking. This is probably the reason why most **eureka moments** come at the least expected time when you take a shower or walk alone.

The recommended dose is only two cups of beer. **Never** drink too much, as it can hamper your performance when you execute your ideas. Although you might be having a rush of creativity, performance is sacrificed.

You should take beer first to get the creative juice flowing. Once you have the ideas, take a glass of coffee to sober you up and induce focus.

BREATH IN, BREATH OUT

Breathing is often taken for granted but has significant impact in our behavior. We breathe fast when we feel anxious and threatened. We breathe deep and slow when we feel relaxed.

The oxygen that is being injected into your bloodstream contributes to the amount of activity in our brain. Too much oxygen can cause our brains to overthink, while small but sufficient amounts can induce our brain to relax and release stress.

Breathing rhythms activate our **sympathetic** and **parasympathetic nervous system**. Rapid shallow breathing stimulates the sympathetic nervous system to enter a fight or flight mode where bodily awareness is at peak. Too much stimulation however, leads to high-blood pressure, stress and anxiety attacks. Slow deep breathing, on the other hand, induces the parasympathetic nervous system to enter a calm and relaxed state.

Learning how to switch between these two modes can help you with productivity.

Deep breathing technique

This method will calm your mind down in order for you to think clearly. Practice this two times a day with small increases in how long you breathe.

1. Prepare your lungs for the exercise by breathing one deep breath. Make sure that your diaphragm is higher than your chest level when you inhale.
2. For 7 seconds, breathe another deep breath **slowly.** Make sure to fill your lungs to its maximum capacity.
3. Release your breath **slowly** for 8 seconds. Completely empty your lungs. Don't release too fast to leave you short of breath nor too slow to have excess gas left in your lungs.
4. Repeat this five times.

If you can recall **NLP** and how switching two pictures can alter mindsets, then you can apply it here. When you breathe in, imagine the positive picture in your mind. And when you breathe out release the negative picture. You can also use words such as "focus" and "anxiety" to make your mind recognize the concepts right away.

Rapid breathing technique

This method, on the other hand, increases brain activity by increasing the oxygen in our brains. Do not overdo this technique for it might lead to hyperventilation.

1. Sit straight and relax your back.
2. Increase your breathing rhythm slowly until you make 2-3 breathing cycles every second. You will feel a bit of strain in your abdominal region. This means that you are now exercising your lungs and increasing its oxygen intake.
3. If this is your first time do not go over 15 seconds. Increase the exercise length by 5 seconds for the succeeding attempts but limit the time to one minute.

The fresh blood that is being injected in your brain will increase its productivity. Your heart will beat faster after this exercise so make sure to settle down for a few seconds before doing anything else.

Our body belongs to us and not the other way around. By using these techniques you can alater your bodily functions depending on your need. You can switch to creative or focused in a few moments. However, only take the recommended length or amount to avoid anything bad happening.

CHAPTER 4.
THINK LIKE A CHAMPION

The world of sports is the testament to man's ability to defy physical limits and achieve the impossible. In boxing, a fighter's ability to keep fighting in spite of being beaten up is called **heart.**

We all have our own way of pushing beyond our capabilities which usually involves motivation. It is no wonder why students could finish so much all in one night, because they have a motivation not to fail. Some employees use their families to psyche themselves up.

These psychological techniques that increase performance and motivation are fields under **Sports Psychology.** The methods used in Sports Psychology can also be applied to normal life. Like athletes, we also lose confidence in ourselves, choke during performances and face tremendous pressure from all sides.

 Success lies not only in building the right goals but also in keeping up the momentum and motivation. Here are six steps to succeed in anything:

1. SET THE RIGHT GOAL

Everything has to start with a goal. It may be long-term or short-term. Regardless of time we need goals to guide us. In constructing your goal you should use the **SMART** model.

Specific- general goals are too broad to achieve. If you have those kind of goals, try cutting them down into small achievable ones.

A common goal is to graduate. There are numerous ways to get there but we need to be specific. A better way to put is "Graduate on time without incurring any failures."

Measureable- your goal must have standards so that you can assess how much you have accomplished and what you need to improve. Common criterions are tangible items and target dates.

Attainable- your ability and determination to accomplish the objective can give you an idea of the attainability of your goal. If you aren't even motivated to start then it might be a good idea to change goals.

Realistic- you should ask yourself if your goal can be done in a real world scenario with lots of factors affecting everything. Take heed of possible delays or changes that you might face while working towards your goal.

Time bound- a deadline to finish will further push you to take action. A lack of a target date will leave you unmotivated. Thus, it might affect your chances of accomplishing your goal.

2. POSITIVE THINKING

Taking time to clear out your mind and then creating a mental image of you succeeding will help you towards your mission. Our discussion on NLP emphasizes how positive and negative thoughts can influence our performance.

Pep yourself up by telling yourself that you can win. Tell yourself what is at stake and think of yourself accomplishing your goal.

Affirmations

Positive affirmations are powerful tools that help you actualize your desires in life. They are encouraging words that you tell yourself when you want to achieve a goal or simply uplift your morale. Each word that boosts your thoughts and actions is all part of positive affirmation.

Modifying your mentality on failure through positive affirmation or utilizing words of encouragement instills significant positive changes in your subconscious mind in order to conquer fear of failing again. When you try to push the subconscious mind to believe that you can do what you desire, you wash away your negative mindset and create a new positive outlook.

Affirmations are usually short, positive statements that aim to resist negative thoughts, feelings, or actions. Thus, positive affirmations are aimed to replace your negative perception that hinders you from believing in yourself.

Since positive affirmations aim to reprogram your patterns of thinking, they transform the way you feel about specific aspects of your life that you want to change. Replacing flawed beliefs with positive ones enables you to achieve positive changes naturally. As such, it will begin reflecting in most aspects of your life as you experience significant, positive changes.

A SIMPLE GUIDE TO LET THE POWER OF POSITIVE AFFIRMATION TRANSFORM YOUR LIFE

First, in a piece of paper, write down the things you desire or want to change in your life. It is recommended to keep it personal instead of sharing it with others. More often than not, family, friends, and society tend to discourage us by saying that things cannot be done. Although they mean well, you need not let their discouraging words enter your thoughts. Once you have written your desire, memorize the positive affirmation and treat it like it already manifested or you have already achieved it.

Next, when you have time in the morning, repeat the affirmation at least 20 times, stating it with passion. Try to imagine yourself with your desire and how your life would be when it manifests into reality. At night, repeat the process prior to going to bed.

Just like Pythagoras insisted that philosophy needed to be a way of life. These positive affirmations that you have written down should be a way of life. Many of Pythagoras followers, implemented the routines very strictly that they became habits.

When you feel doubtful about your desire, clear your mind and repeat the affirmation. Discard all negative thoughts that hinder your focus from acquiring your desire.

Finally, keep your mind open to opportunities. The means of achieving your desire may not come as you have imagined them to be. Thus, you need to be alert to opportunities and take action upon them.

EXAMPLES OF POSITIVE AFFIRMATIONS FOR COMMON ISSUES

Affirmations for Action (Motivation)

All of my actions reveal my intentions.

My actions are geared toward my aspirations.

My actions support my desires or goals.

I bring positive outcome into my life through taking positive actions.

I take goal-directed actions each day.

Affirmations for Love

I give out love and love will return to me multiplied.

I deserve love and I accept it now.

I rejoice the love I receive each day.

Affirmations for Peace and Harmony

I trust the process of life.

All my relationships are harmonious.

I am at peace with myself and others.

Affirmations for Joy and Happiness

I choose joy, love, and freedom and allow favorable things to transpire in my life.

Life is full of delightful surprises.

My life is filled with fund, joy, friendship, and love.

I choose to relax, forgive, stop all criticism, and be open.

3. ACTION!

After setting up your goal and mentally preparing yourself, it's time to take action. Keep yourself motivated and determined to finish. Avoid procrastination and make the most out of every minute.

Remember to always take a break in between long periods of work. Use your break as a motivation for you to work harder. Tell yourself that you will devote 10 minutes to social media **once you finish** a part of your work.

After refreshing yourself, go back in and work again.

4. PRAISE AND REWARD

Once you meet your quota for the day, treat yourself to something you like. It could be a cup of beer or some time watching the television. Let yourself feel that you deserve the break because you worked so hard.

Tell yourself how good you've performed that day. Giving yourself compliments while in front of the mirror can boost self-esteem.

5. REFLECT

Before going to sleep, grab a journal and record everything that happened today. List down the reasons why you did good today. After that, enumerate the various challenges that you had to overcome in order to finish. Be specific of what the challenges are, for it will make it easier for you to adjust the following day. Close the journal entry by giving yourself a positive message and by setting the objectives needed to be done the next day.

6. MOVING ON

The following day, pick up your journal again and read the last part. Reflect again what the problems were last time and figure out a way to get through them. Move on if you weren't able to do well yesterday. If you did well then encourage yourself to improve even better.

CHAPTER 5.

INTERACTING WITH OTHER CULTURES AND SOCIETIES

It's amazing how the human species could be so diverse. We share the same genetic makeup but we don't behave the same. Our upbringing and background has certainly contributed to this. Thus, talking to people from other countries poses as a challenge.

Since we are different in upbringing, certainly we have different views or perception about life.

The field of Social Psychology studies how our thoughts and behaviors are altered by people around us. On the other hand, Cultural Psychology studies how social constructs and ideals affect our way of living.

Social Psychology is more focused on the interaction that happens between people. While Cultural Psychology studies in depth why cultures and traditions affect humans.

Understanding concepts from both sciences will increase our awareness about human diversity. The first part of this chapter will tackle Social Psychology while the other half will focus on Cultural Psychology.

ATTITUDES AND PERSUASION

Social Psychology is often confused with Sociology since they both study group norms and behavior. Social Psychology focuses on the individual while Sociology delves on the group.

One of the main pillars of Social Psychology are the concepts of attitudes and persuasion. We interact with each other every day. We use communication as an instrument to ask people to help us. We **persuade** others to change their **attitudes** so that they can help us. Attitudes are pre-existing ideals of an individual such as preference. And the way we alter attitudes is called **persuasion.**

In the business world these two concepts are key in managing people or enticing consumers to buy your products.

Although people change attitudes because of logical arguments based on facts, other factors come into play in the game of persuasion. People are also influenced by a person's physical attractiveness, voice modulation, gestures and even posture.

Social Psychology theorize that our actions whether verbal or non-verbal have significant effects with our interaction.

During a job interview your goal is to **persuade** the employer to hire you. Even before you speak the first few seconds are critical. In corporate meetings your appearance can affect your credibility.

The following are tips how to persuade people to change their attitudes:

1. SMILE

The moment you meet with someone, the smile is the first feature that is noticed. It's surprising how a few mouth muscles can help you win over people.

The attribution theory explains that people give certain attributes to others depending on characteristics they possess. A smile attributes a person to warm and friendly, while a frown associates a person as sad and unapproachable.

Don't fake your smile. Use your mouth muscles to create a natural and pleasant smile. Match it by relaxing your facial muscles especially in the eye region.

2. POSTURE

A straight body connotes an air of confidence which is associated with credibility. Train your body to walk and sit straight by practicing it at home. Create a mental note so that you'll always be aware.

3. VOICE MODULATION

Even the manner of how you say things can persuade others. Change your tone to emphasize key points that you want to be remembered. Avoid stuttering as it can show that you are not prepared. Don't speak too fast nor too slow because you have to match the tempo of your message. If your message is positive then an ecstatic tone is good. If the message is negative a firm and serious tone is appropriate.

UNDERSTANDING CULTURE AND SOCIAL NORMS

When people converge and live together, they create similar behaviors among themselves. Cultures are manmade objectives and norms for the benefit of the many. Living in a community requires everyone to work hand-in-hand. Since everyone has grown in various lands with different climate and geography, varying cultures are created.

The culture we were brought up to changes our **worldview.** A change in worldview dictates our **perceptions.** From our perceptions the community creates values that are important. From the priorities that we set, we then adjust our behavior to meet those objectives.

When you go to another country it is recommended to know their culture. Here are the five dimensions of culture that you should know:

INDIVIDUALISM VS. COLLECTIVISM

Countries like the US are **individualistic.** They highly value personal independence. To succeed, you need to stand on your own two feet otherwise you'll not survive. This perception about sustenance is egotistic for people under this culture prioritizes personal needs before societal ones.

Collectivism emphasizes that one cannot survive without the help of others. A flourishing community means that individuals enjoy a good life. In this context, children are brought up to become interdependent upon each other.

COMMUNICATION: DIRECT VS. INDIRECT

Directly implying your message by using straightforward words is direct communication. Countries under this culture value conciseness and clarity to avoid misunderstanding.

Cultures that prioritize harmony and friendship **implies** indirectly their message. People in this context would rather politely nod, than argue with.

LOCUS OF CONTROL: INTERNAL VS. EXTERNAL

How people perceive the environment either as a figure that influences their action or as an entity that can be changed is called Locus of Control.

Countries that have an Internal Locus of Control perception, think that the environment, aside from a few fundamental concepts, can be changed to benefit them. People with this view hold themselves accountable for both their failures and successes.

Other cultures hold life as **fatalistic.** Countries under this think that their lives are already pre-determined before they were born. Their External Locus of Control perception emphasize that their environment is a critical factor in their future.

CLASHING VIEWS ON UNCERTAINTY AND CHANCE

Opportunists are most likely to have a **positive view on uncertainty and chance.** They thrive in improving themselves, even if it means failing. Changes that can make life more convenient for them are readily accepted.

People who would rather stick to tradition and be conservative have a **skeptical view.** They highly encourage sticking to societal norms that have been proven by time to be effective. Change is somehow avoided for it will cause chaos and dissonance.

TIME: MONOCHROMIC VS. POLYCHROMIC

A **monochromic view** on time suggests that we should all do things one at a time. One key concept in this culture is how time is viewed as a limited resources. Therefore, efficiency is needed to achieve every task. This culture believes that no interference or unforeseen circumstances should hamper the progress of work.

A culture under the **Polychromic view** holds time as a tool. Time under this perception is unlimited. People who work with this view go with the flow. They accept circumstances and adjust. They also **multitask** when they work.

After learning these concepts you will easily adjust with other people regardless of where they come from. Using the techniques applied in Social Psychology you can effectively communicate with other while adjusting to their cultures and views.

CHAPTER 6.

FROM APES AND BEYOND: HOW EVOLUTION HAS CHANGED OUR BEHAVIOR

Our defining characteristics that make us human was brought about by thousands of years of evolution.

Evolutionary Psychology sheds new light on some of our behavior. From our communities to fears, evolution could explain the mysteries that we have pondered on for a long time.

THE RISE OF COMMUNITIES AND SOCIETY

Protohumans, our great ancestors, lived in an unforgiving environment. Predators were a constant threat and the climate was just as deadly. To maximize the chance of survival, our ancestors bonded together to create a community.

The members of this community were assigned different task that will help everyone. Men were in charge of hunting for food. While women settled in their homes to care for the young.

Up until now this still holds true. This might explain why men feel obligated to get a job while women have maternal instincts to care for children.

Since men were keeping the family alive this led to a patriarchal society and ultimately became the origin of sexism.

ALTRUISM

One surprising trait of humans is the capacity to sacrifice gain for the benefit of others. But this is expected to give a return of favor in the future. Altruism runs under the concept of "you scratch my back, and I scratch yours."

Altruism is a trust system, and that violation of this trust by cheating will cause you to be left out. This possible punishment was a deterrent enough for members to be obedient.

In today's society, we do other's favor at the expense of our convenience. We build friendship amongst ourselves. A harmonious relationship with others will make it easier for us to gain a favor in the future.

RACE RECOGNITION

Racism is strictly frowned upon in many countries. But it might be possible that racial profiling was the manifestation of people interacting with other races. Protohumans used body features like skin color, facial figures and voice accents as signs of membership from a race.

In ancient times, people with different races came together and made alliances. Protohumans used their races to distinguish who is part of what clan.

Now, we can quickly identify a person's race or ethnicity by checking their bodily characteristics. Racism might have arose from outsiders joining communities. Obviously, outsiders wouldn't have received the same benefits that the majority enjoy.

SIGNIFICANCE TO PSYCHOLOGICAL DISORDERS

Phobias, anxiety and other psychological conditions might have been a manifestation of evolution.

Our ancestors faced various dangers while hunting. A fear of tigers and lions have triggered a flight-or-fight response for us to stay alive. During this period of awareness, our hearts beats faster, we experience anxiety and we think critically. Although threats are now reduced, phobias are still there.

A condition called postpartum depression, wherein a mother feels saddened after giving childbirth, might be caused by failed expectations.

Harsh conditions and limited resources made child-rearing difficult. Therefore, feeding a child is an investment under the assumption that in the future the child will contribute to the family.

If the child had defects or deformities a mother will feel depressed over the resources she has to make to keep the baby alive. The treatment for this condition is through depressants, but counselling and psychoanalytic therapy are better alternatives. Helping the mother understand her baby's state will make her capable of raising the child.

These are just some of the theories that have contributed to our human behavior and thought. But right now, because of our changing world, it won't be long before these behaviors change once more.

PRACTICAL ADVICE:

The Road to Success

You need a clear definition of success in order to take hold of it. While success may be different things to different people, it generally involves continuous improvement in the quality of the life you live.

In order to continuously improve your life, you need to understand that improvement must be consistent, and that you do not define any moment as the day or hour where you stop striving to become more successful. As long as you live, you will strive to become better and you will find joy in doing just that. Remember, there is always room for "more." There is always room to become "better," – even if it were just to have a little more or to become a little better.

Seek improvement in all the areas of your life – spiritual, emotional, physical, mental and social. Take note of your long-term and short-term goals for each of these areas, and on daily, weekly, monthly, quarterly and yearly bases, take a little time off to evaluate how you have improved, and how you have moved closer towards achieving your goals.

Your spiritual improvement will let you add meaning to your life. It will encourage you, and push you to know that there is more to life other than yourself. Your spiritual improvement will keep steadfast in your faith and in your values.

The previous chapter has talked about emotions and how they affect you. Keep in mind that it will be a constant challenge to keep your emotions under control, but when you learn to do this, you will value it highly. You will learn to recognize your inner strength and take pride in it. Others will notice it too, and they will admire you for it.

In the course of achieving your goals, never neglect your physical health and improvement. Aim to become stronger, to become more fit and to look better. This has a wonderful effect on your self-esteem. Set specific and measurable goals for your physical fitness.

For mental health, continuously test your creativity. Never stop learning. Be inquisitive. Write down your insights. Use your knowledge to improve the overall quality of your life. Share your ideas with others, and as you learn about other people's ideas, continue to develop your own.

The quality of your social life – the relationships that you have with those who matter most to you, will influence much of your actions. And since other people will influence your identity, it is best to surround yourself with optimistic and successful individuals.

COMMITTING TO CONTINUOUS IMPROVEMENT

Taking action can be a one-time event, but if it's like that, there should be no expectation to see a significant improvement in your life. The challenge of lasting success is the ability to consistently improve.

In other words, what you need is an ID: *Improvement Daily.* Always ask the following questions:

1. What can I do better today?
2. How can I be a better person today?
3. What area of my life can I further improve?
4. What can I do differently right now?
5. What significant contribution can I make at work? In my family? In my community?

Learn to make each day count. Look at your past with thankfulness at what it taught you, and with pride at what success it gave you. Visualize your future with amazement at what you can become. Enjoy your present, knowing that it is a result of your past, and a springboard for your future success.

ASKING GOOD QUESTIONS

We all engage in self-thought and ask questions for ourselves. The questions we ask dictate our focus, and greatly influence our perspectives, as well as our actions.

One practice you need to develop is asking good questions. Good questions are those that empower you. They let you think out of the box, look at solutions and gain different perspectives. They enable you to take a look at your resources, your abilities, and the potential in everything – potential from you, from others and from your environment. They make you look at possibilities. They are the "what if" questions – the same questions which the world's innovators asked, and which helped them create great things.

You will know that you are asking the right questions when in your quest to answer them, you come up with more ideas, and you get to focus on what you can do, instead of what can't be done. Such questions will give you your eureka moments, and they will provide learning and development.

You know you are asking the wrong questions when the answers you get from them lead you to blame, self-guilt, frustration, anger and depression. The wrong questions get you stuck, and make you feel that there is nothing you can do. When the questions you ask keep bringing about more problems than solutions, then you know that you are asking bad questions.

When you start being negative and ask, "Why can't I…" instead of "What can I do to…" then you need to pause, re-examine your thoughts and rephrase your question.

MAKING A DIFFERENCE

Grand words like "revolutionary," "innovative," "state of the art," and "unique" are all derived from the idea of making a difference.

It is in your hands to make your life worthwhile. As you press towards your goal, remember to make a difference – the good kind of difference – not only in your life, but also in other people's lives. You will get a lot of insights by working with other people, and you will also get fulfillment.

There is no one else who is exactly like you. There is only one "you," so you are more than capable of being different. The impact of your contribution depends on your passion, your action, your perseverance, and your ability to ask good questions.

More Notes to Apply

The one thing everyone wants is happiness.

Everyone wants to be happy, but not everyone knows or understands its secret. Do you know how to be happy?

With resources, a person can feel temporarily happy or pleasant. Taking drugs, acquiring material wealth and possessions, having companionship, going on adventures and eating great food can all leave pleasant sensations that are closely associated to how happiness feels like. As you can see from these examples, most of our ways to obtain happiness greatly depend on our external environment. However, you already know the truth about the external environment: you can influence it, but you do not have total control over it. Disaster can strike any time, taking away everything that you have. So then, what happens to your happiness?

The norm about happiness is this: it is a result. Happiness is an "if" statement, and so there are conditions to being happy. If you are successful, you will be happy. If you have something or someone, you will be happy. If this is your perspective on happiness, then I guarantee that it will be quite a tiring journey for you, because you will keep on wanting more, and you will find that happiness is quick and fleeting.

To make happiness last, this is how you define it – you define happiness as an inexhaustible resource that is already available to you. As long as you're around, you possess happiness within you. And it is what you will use to achieve. It is what you will use to have someone or something. Happiness is your drive. Your happiness shapes your decisions, and it will be your focus. You don't do things to be happy. You are a happy person to begin with, and that is why you live. This is happiness defined outside your environment. This is what it means to say that happiness is an attitude.

MANAGING MEANINGS

Your reality is shaped by the meanings you attach to it. Any event can be viewed positively or negatively. In the same way that you can choose to be thankful daily, you can also choose to be depressed about not having more.

If you spilled coffee on your clothes, you can feel angry about how you made a stupid mistake and how you will look terrible for the rest of the day. Or, you can also feel thankful that you've at least got something to wear, and that you did not hurt yourself in the process.

By managing the meanings you create in life, you bring about the happiness inside you. When you are challenged, ask yourself how you can use the situation to your advantage. If you lose your job, think about what you have learned from it. Think about what you can do. Perhaps it is time for you to find a new job or start your own business.

Do not let other people define your life's meanings, because then, you will be depending on your external environment again. Take criticisms constructively, acknowledge other people's opinions, but know within yourself that your ultimate success lies in living happily each day. For every day that you refuse to be happy, you *lose the game* and *you fail the test.* You miss out on life.

So develop this happy attitude. Nurture a happy soul. Let your thoughts be positive. Use words which communicate joy. Instead of seeking to judge people, learn to understand them. Let your mind and body both exhibit happiness.

BECOMING BETTER

Your happiness will not be an excuse for you to slack off. Remember: the key is for you to use your happiness as a source of your strength, as a reliable motivation for you to become better. As you read through the last sections of this book, develop your skill at mastering happiness. If you constantly make happiness a habit, you will see that the way you create meanings will change, and your life will greatly improve.

ANTICIPATION

One of the things that can set you apart from everyone else is *anticipation.* It is anticipation that can put you ahead of your time. If you can observe closely enough to be able to see what people will value, then you will anticipate possible problems, and you will also anticipate possible solutions. Anticipation is about going beyond possible reactions. It is about being able to make the necessary preparations for possible outcomes.

Anticipation is quite a rare skill, because people tend to prefer to react and solve problems as they come. Sometimes, you get so confident about what you can already do and think that since it has always worked in the past, it will continue to work for you in the future. Note, however, that this is not the right way to think things over, because everything changes constantly. Who would have thought that film cameras will be easily outdated by digital photography? Or that beepers will be made obsolete by mobile phones? Businesses that fail to anticipate new technologies that can replace their product or service cannot expect to last very long, and this is what you need to do in life. You need to anticipate.

INNOVATION

Anticipation makes you the type of person who does not simply react or respond to changes. It makes you see what changes are coming, and prepare for them even if they had not happened yet. But what if you become the initiator of change?

Another way for you to channel your strength and happiness into something productive is by choosing to be an innovator. As an innovator, you will create new ways of doing things; you will not merely improve or create better versions.

More Books by Jonny Bell:

SOCIOLOGY:

A PRACTICAL UNDERSTANDING OF WHY WE DO WHAT WE DO

Preview of Book:

CHAPTER 1. A BRIEFING TO HUMAN BEHAVIOR

We tend to respond to each situation differently. One may cry at a movie while another may laugh at it. One may get angry at an offensive joke while others may not feel anything about it. Some may have a different degree of sense of sacrifice and may do a little bit more in order to progress to an endeavor while others may just simply give up at the first sign of difficulty. Experts believe that human behavior cannot be explained by one cause simply because human behavior is caused by multiple interconnected things or events.

THE THREE ASPECTS OF HUMAN BEHAVIOR

THE ANIMAL WITHIN US THAT IS "ID"

When we are first born, void of the ability to reason out and without the concept of how the external world operates, we, as babies, operate by the mechanism of "id" or "it", as it is often correlated with our animalistic or base desires.

In psychoanalytic theory, "id" is the part of human consciousness that is said to be the reservoir of the instinctual behaviors or drives of an individual. These primitive behaviors, like human urges and sexual desires, operate through the "pleasure principle". Because it operates by the principle of pleasure, the "id" requires immediate gratification. Id disregards what is realistic, logical or moral. Because id represents a collection of urges, it is said to have no real awareness of the outside world.

When we are hungry or thirsty, and our actions and our plans are directed towards meeting this need, then we know that the id component of our consciousness is in charge. The id is important in our lives because it represents our body's needs. It influences our minds and our behaviors by exerting pressure upon it and gives a feeling of release, through pleasure, when our urges are fulfilled. According to Sigmund Freud, id is the primary source of almost all psychic energy, thus, making it the primary component of our personalities.

EGO: THE MEDIATOR OF OUR BEHAVIOR

Between the second or third year, the second portion of the mind develops. By this stage, the upper portion of the id or "I", which is located both on the preconscious and conscious level, is modified by the outside world forming a component of a person's personality that is capable of dealing with reality.

During the development of a person's consciousness, a person may realize that his or her desires and urges cannot always be fulfilled. The ego, then, controls how much of the id's desires and urges are allowed to be expressed. Unlike id, which operates on the "pleasure principle", ego operates on the "reality principle". Ego allows a person to act upon an urge or impulse, or abandon it altogether, by allowing the principle of reality to weigh in the costs and benefits of an action. Unlike id which acts on the animalistic drives, the ego is able to use the thinking faculty. It is able to observe the outside world and decides its next course of action based on what is rational and realistic. In most cases, the desires and urges that were allowed to be expressed are satisfied through delayed gratification. That is, the urge or impulse is allowed to be expressed only at an appropriate time or place.

Whenever we feel like buying something, and we decide not to because the money we should use to purchase it is needed for other things, and we abandon that desire, the ego part of our consciousness is at work. The "id" part of our consciousness tells us to buy something out of an impulse or an instant liking to a thing.

SUPEREGO: THE STRICT MORALIST

When we reach the age of 5, a portion of the ego is modified through the internalization of moral standards and ideals acquired from our family, from the society and from organized religious groups. The superego controls our behavior by giving us the sense of what is right and what is wrong.

Whenever we do things that we think are wrong, based on what we have learned, superego punishes us with the feeling of guilt. Whenever we do things that are right, based on the set of rules we learned, the superego rewards us with the feeling of pride. Like the id, the superego disregards what is real or observable and desires moral perfection. The id and the superego are always in conflict to control our behavior. It is up to the ego to mediate between these two aspects of human consciousness. Ego decides which one should be expressed.

Whenever the id aspect of our personality is dominant, we tend to do things that are destructive or illogical (and oftentimes, immoral). Similarly, whenever our superego is dominant, we tend to be perfectionists and strict moralists.

MORALITY: A GUIDE AND A BASIS FOR HUMAN BEHAVIOR

Society, guided by religion and superstitious beliefs, has always devised rules. The principle concerned with the difference between what is right and what is wrong and that which defines what is a good and a bad behavior is called morality. However, the definition of what is good or bad and what is right or wrong has not always been an easy issue. The scope of the topic involving the comprehensive definition of morality— where it begins and ends, to what group does it apply, how much is the influence of religion, etc.—is beyond the concern of this book. However, a new definition of it based from new literatures on morality states that morality is anything which pertains to the happiness, well-being, or suffering of conscious creatures or entities and anything that has something to do with saving or ending a conscious life. Some societies, however, have a different viewpoint on morality. Others have set the standards and definitions of what is right and what is wrong based on the predominant idea of the many.

However vague the definition of morality, it is evidently the very source of the energy of our superego. The effects of these sets of rules are so great that an individual who thinks that he violated them would inflict self-punishment, event to the point of suicide, because of a feeling of guilt imposed by super ego.

CHAPTER 2. WHY IS HUMAN BEHAVIOR DIFFICULT TO EXPLAIN?

The interplay, alone, of the three components of our behavior and our personality, namely the id, ego and super ego, renders human behavior complex and indeterminate. At some point, depending on such conditions as mood, physical need, or uncontrolled impulse, the id and the super ego could enter into a heated battle which will be manifested as expressions of human behavior—often, that which is not seen to be expressed normally by the person.

Experts agree that human behavior is caused by many things and we cannot, therefore, explain human behavior through a single cause. Factors considered to be the cause of human behavior are those that are both internal and external. When we say internal, we refer to the condition of our consciousness—that is, whether or not ego is able to mediate between id and super ego. If not, another factor would have to be that component which is dominant—id or superego. When we speak of external factors, we speak of the events that could bring about stress. Our stress reaction and response could also play a vital role in how we think and how our thoughts manifest into action.

FACTORS THAT AFFECT HUMAN BEHAVIOR

Behavior is an acquired human attribute. The behavior we have today is the result of the effect of various factors on our behavior. Some factors may be in conflict with another in shaping our behavior, but most often, the most dominant factor gets to shape how we assess and respond to situations, how we react to certain stimulus, how we solve a problem and how we deal with other human beings.

1. ROLE

Our roles in the society, be it as a politician, a prisoner, a vendor, a criminal, a priest, a person of authority or any role for that matter regulates and determines our expressed behavior. Each social situation or environment has its own set of expectations about how it is to behave properly. We tend to conform to this expectation as much as possible and this very process of conforming to this expectation greatly shapes our behaviors.

2. RESOURCES

Imagine being in a dangerous situation say, in a burning building. The availability of resources determines our behavior in that situation. Are there exitways? Are you assured of your safety? Can you hear the sirens signaling rescue? Can you still breathe?

The availability of resources during a particular time determines how we respond. Our responses, which then turn to behavior, are determined by how well we react to stressors.

3. HABITS AND AUTOMATIC RESPONSES

Whenever our lives go into autopilot mode, patterned behavior as brushing our teeth before we sleep, the common phrase we say whenever we are surprised, or saying thank you whenever offered something or sorry whenever we err, we form and act out a habit.

Habits or wonts are behavioral routines that tend to be imbedded into us and are acted out subconsciously, or that which needs no conscious thought. It is thought to be acquired through repetition. What is astonishing about the "habit" aspect of our behavior is that the brain expends almost no energy performing it. It creates a simple neural pathway which tends to be the only brain activity during the execution of a habitual act.

Experts agree that habit starts with a pattern called a habit loop. This pattern is a three-part process. The first part involves a cue or trigger. Whenever this trigger is present, the brain enters an automatic mode and the behavior is manifested. Second is the routine which is the behavior itself. The third step is the reward or something that will motivate the brain to remember the habit.

4. *KNOWLEDGE AND EXPERIENCE*

History and experience influence how we react to a particular situation. People who have experienced something and have successfully gone through it will more likely be capable of resolving the same situation in the future. It is identified by many as "growth" and that is the main reason why experienced and older people tend to deal with a situation more effectively than inexperienced individuals can.

5. BELIEFS

The set of beliefs and principles imposed or taught to us by our family, church and/or the society forms a great part or our id. It determines what is right and wrong and what we should achieve and not. These set of beliefs are encoded into us through the concept of punishment and reward. Often, the punishment is rejection and the reward of social acceptance. The degree for which these beliefs are encoded into us determines the strength or our super ego. Consequently, the strength of our super ego, determined by these sets of moral rules, determines how well we manage our id or our basal urges.

6. EMOTIONS

Experts are yet to unravel the exact purpose of emotions to humans. Whatever is the exact purpose of our emotions, one thing is for sure. Humans are more likely bound to act in response to emotion. Our emotions tend to influence our behavior greatly. When we are in a positive mood, we tend to be optimistic with the results of our endeavor and decide to pursue it. When we are angry, we tend to let go of what is logical and disregard the requisites for proper behavior and we tend to act irrationally and speak unacceptable words. When we are sad, we tend to be pessimistic and lose the energy and the drive to do things.

7. *HORMONES*

If super ego is formed and bolstered by how well our beliefs is established and encoded into us, id is bolstered by our hormonal component. Hormones are chemicals produced by the body to perform specific tasks. They are considered the silent drivers of human personality and behavior. They determine many aspects of human behavior such as aggression, appetite and attraction. When a particular hormone surges through the body, its effect (or side effect) is manifested through a desire or urge that requires release or satisfaction.

8. *PRE-NATAL*

New studies reveal that humans are particularly susceptible to conditioning during development inside the mother's womb. The presence and absence of certain hormones in the mother's bloodstream, the emotional state and stress level of a mother, as well as the mother's diet all influence the behavior of a child. Feeding instinct, homosexuality and preferences are some of the aspects of human behavior that develop, through conditioning, during pregnancy and at birth.

9. GENETICS AND EPIGENETICS

Studies reveal that just as the nurture aspect of the external world (i.e. role, resources, habit and experience) influences human behavior, so does the nature aspect or the genetic makeup. Although the genetic makeup of every human differs from another by roughly 0.5%, genes, hailed as the building blocks of life, greatly determine our physical propensity and our behavioral tendencies.

Another aspect of genetics, a separate and equally different discipline, the epigenetics, is gaining popularity among experts. Epigenetics is a discipline that deals with the inheritable changes that happen in gene activity which are not caused by a change in DNA sequence. Changes in gene expression, or changes that allow a part of the gene to be suppressed or expressed, determine the differences in the behavior of two humans with similar genetic makeup.

Applied Psychology

CHAPTER 3. WE DON'T ALWAYS DO WHAT WE WANT TO DO

Read more

ONE LAST THING...

If you enjoyed this book or found it useful I'd be very grateful if you'd post a short review on Amazon. Your support really does make a difference and I read all the reviews personally so I can get your feedback and make this book even better.

Thanks again for your support!